UNEXPLAI
Yet
UNDENIABLE

BY

DANIELE LUCIANO MOSKAL

PUBLISHED BY
UNIQUE WRITING PUBLICATIONS

PO Box 2338
Leagrave LUTON LU4 0YQ GREAT BRITAIN.

UNIQUE WRITING PUBLICATIONS

The aims of Unique Writing Publications are too:

Teach and proclaim, God's uncompromising Word with excellence, by revealing the very mind of God, to the body of Christ (the Church), through the printed Word, by publishing unique inspirational Christian writers.

For further information, please write to:

UNIQUE WRITING PUBLICATIONS
PO Box 2338
Leagrave
LUTON
LU4 0YQ
GREAT BRITAIN.

UNEXPLAINABLE YET UNDENIABLE

CONTENTS PAGE

Editor's Word of Thanks.

To my one and only love, Jesus my Lord and Saviour, My Inspiration and Aspiration, --- I give You all my praise, honour and thanksgiving for the leading of Your precious Holy Spirit, (the teacher of all Teachers), who continues to open the windows of my mind with biblical truth, wisdom and knowledge. Thank You for saving me and giving me the anointed tongue and ear of the learned man to speak and teach Your living Word to the hungry souls who feed on Your daily bread. Ose Baba! Thank You Father God Almighty, for stirring up my gift, in Jesus' magnificent name!!

The object of this book, written over a period of years, is to declare the plain and simple "Gospel" in an easy-to-comprehend tone of voice, encouraging and urging the reader to embrace Christ who is freely offered to all mankind in His glorious gospel.
A symposium of nine topics is not easy to edit or to produce; and so I start this preface by expressing a personal gratitude to my beautiful anointed wife, Moji Moskal who shepherded this project in prayers and exercised her patience in helping to get my books into print. HONEY, I love you! You are God's very special gift to me, enabling ministry to others.

Pastor Daniel, loves you!

A big THANK YOU for your support, encouragement, and assisting me during the preparation of the final manuscript.

I would also like to express my sincere appreciation to all Christian authors world-wide, especially for their vision of teaching and sharing biblical-based, uncompromising faith at every opportunity. I pray that you teachers of the Word of God, will continue to have a servant-oriented lifestyle. May you always stir up your gifts, refine your concepts, values and skills God presents to you and encourage one another to publish the Truth of the 'Living Word' for the benefit of others. I end this preface by acknowledging certain people who have been a tremendous blessing in my life.

ACKNOWLEDGMENTS

I would like to express my very special thanks to:
My late Mother and Father (Kassymr & Mafalda Moskal) , I love you and miss you so very, very much. My brother Mario and my three sisters Trudy, Veronica & Olga (the Twins). My nieces, Faye, Rebecca and Carla, and my dear nephew Kassy (number two), and the rest of my family Italian and Nigerian world-wide.

Pastor Andy Wall (pastor to Pastors) and members of 'Grace Christian International Centre', who have blessed me with their encouragement, wisdom and prayers.

Evangelist/Pastor Peter and Julie Gabriel of 'PRAISETEK' for their support, but even more for being good friends.

Ms Florrie Brown, a true friend who loves at all times. You're a blessed woman of God - thank you for always being there for me and my family.

Not forgetting all the the congregation members of "Rivers of Life" Church (Luton); especially all the prayer warriors of the Youth Ministry. Daddy Loves you!!!

Victor & Bola (Congratulations). Thank you for all your prayers, and telephone calls!

Oak Hill Bible/Theological College & Middlesex University.
Mr & Mrs Roy Walker and all the helpful staff at 'King Print' (Luton) for your printing and production expertise.

FOREWORD

Christ Jesus came into this world to save sinners, which includes you and me (all of us). Most other religions will try to point the way to God, but Jesus said, *"I am, the Way, the Truth, and the Life. No one comes to the father except through Me"* ~ **John 14.6**

Or as someone once said: 'If all other religions are correct then Jesus Christ is correct, and if Jesus Christ is correct, then all the other religions are wrong! Right?

Jesus Christ of Nazareth alone was sinless. he alone was big enough to carry on His shoulders and pay for the sin of the whole world as He died on the Cross at Calvary Hill. Only he and He alone can forgive a man, a woman, a child (any person) and bring them back to God.

He is simply *UNEXPLAINABLE YET UNDENIABLE!*

Today, it is possible to visit the graves of some of the world's greatest religious and political leaders. Jesus Christ too, was also buried, but three days later by God's unexplainable yet undeniable power, He rose from the dead. There is an empty tomb where Jesus Christ once laid. Now resurrected Christ rises above the rest of humanity and surpasses all other leaders. For only He alone can establish a relationship between us and God.

religion is humanity's sincere desire, but a vain attempt to reach God. Christ Jesus is God's only bridge from us to Him.

For Jesus was the only person born to die, and die for us. The

Holy bible says,

"Neither is there salvation in any other, for there is no other name under heaven given among men by which we must be saved" ~ **Acts 4:12.**

Christ's death is Unexplainable yet Undeniable, yet His death was absolutely vital, because it is the only way you and I can know God and experience everlasting life.

The Holy Bible says,

"For to this end Christ died and rose and lived again that He might be the LORD of both the dead and the living." ~ **Romans 14.9.**

This book was written over a period of years after my own encounter with Jesus Christ. I experienced His Unexplainable yet Undeniable power late one evening back in November 1993.

My 'upper-room' experience was quite simply Unexplainable yet Undeniable. I could not explain to you in simplistic terms of vocabulary what happened that wonderful evening, but I cannot deny His awesome ressurection power that supernaturally transformed my entire life into a new 'born-again' child of the true and living God.

For you the reader of this book, I do not know where you are at this present moment in time concerning your faith or what you believe in. But, with my little experience or education about the power of the ressurected Christ, I know for certain that most books found in modern libraries world-wide for example;- History; Archaeology; Science, even the Holy Quaran, and not forgetting the Holy Bible mention in one form or another that Jesus Christ of Nazareth rose from the dead.

This concludes that Jesus, HIS story and the extraordinary experience of Apostle Paul of Tarsus, had road to Damascus, and my very own personal encounter with Jesus Christ is simply

UNEXPLAINABLE YET UNDENIABLE!!

Pastor Daniele Luciano Moskal

JESUS, HIS story

JESUS, <u>HIS</u> story

INTRODUCTION

All that is known of the man Jesus of Nazareth appears in the first four Gospel books of Matthew, Mark, Luke, and John which are found in the New Testament. Four hundred years had passed now, since the prophet Malachi had predicted the day of the second Elijah, would precede the LORD'S coming and nothing new was added to the Holy Bible.

God's prophets had fallen silent. During this period of silence, Middle Eastern empires of military power and wealth rose and fell, and the small nation of Israel suffered under the domination of superior powers like Greece and Rome.

Then, suddenly something miraculous occurred. A baby boy was born to a young Jewish couple, in a small cowshed in Bethlehem of Judea, in the days of King Herod. A boy who would grow up in a humble town called Nazareth --- a baby unlike any who had never been born previously --- a baby who was to have such a great influence on world history. A baby born to a young virgin, Jewish girl called, Mary and her betrothed husband Joseph. And Jewish history, would witness a love-story, a story of everlasting love that no man, woman or child had ever read, heard or witnessed ever before. The child's name was **JESUS**, (*Yeshua*), "because He would save His people from their sins."

The Jews especially, and people all over the world had been eagerly awaiting the **"Messiah"**, **"The Christ"** (*Greek*), " **the**

Anointed One" (*Hebrew*). Could this Jesus, the son of a Jewish carpenter be the deliverer, the illumination and aspiring hope to all mankind? Could this man Jesus, be the only bridge between God and man?

Was Isaiah the Old Testament prophet correct, when he prophesied about a "*suffering servant*", was he really talking about Jesus, or another man who would come from Israel to bring light to all nations in chapter 53 of his book? The prophet also spoke: "*that a virgin would be with child and will give birth to a son, and will call him Emmanuel (Emmanuel means God is with us)*." **ISAIAH 8:14.**

Was, Isaiah talking about Jesus?

To answer the above questions, one needs to look closely at the extraordinary life of Jesus of Nazareth, His death by crucifixion to make your own personal mind, to who Jesus really was in History….

The Gospels of Matthew and Luke, in the New Testament, begin with the birth of Jesus to a Jewish virgin named Mary. The Gospels of Mark and John, begin with events that took place some thirty years later. Generally though, the life-story of Jesus of Nazareth, is much the same in all Four Gospels.

Jesus was born in Bethlehem, the town of King David around Judea in the days of King Herod, probably around 6 B.C. Little or if anything is mentioned of Jesus' childhood, except that he lived and grew up in a village called Nazareth in the province of

Galilee with his parents, Mary and Joseph. Joseph worked as a carpenter, skilled in making such things as cattle yokes, chests, bins, beds and kneading troughs. And as a young boy, Jesus probably served as his helper. The common language of the Jews was Aramaic, and in his home Jesus would have spoken this language. The synagogue served both as his school and his place of worship. Here Jesus would have studied the Scriptures of old Prophets, and probably learned his prayers in the ancient Hebrew tongue. However we are told in the Gospel of Luke that during his youth, *"the child (Jesus) grew and became strong; he was filled with wisdom and the grace of God was upon him"* (2:40 NIV).

Jesus was thirty years of age when John the Baptist began preaching in the valley of the Jordan near the Dead Sea. John was believed to be a Prophet, and many people came in large numbers to listen to what he was preaching. They came from Galilee, and from the surrounding provinces of Palestine, and among them was Jesus who for a number of days had listened to the preaching messages of John. John preached a Baptism of Repentance for the forgiveness of sins, quoting the words of the Prophet Isaiah one of the Old Testament messengers of God:

"A voice of one calling in the desert,
Prepare the way for the LORD,
Make straight paths for Him,
Every valley shall be filled in, every mountain and hill made low.
The crooked roads shall become straight, the rough ways smooth.
And all mankind will see God's salvation." (40:3-5)

John told the people to repent, to turn away from their sinful living, for the Kingdom of Heaven was at hand. Those who repented, John baptised to start a new life in the LORD. Jesus himself was approximately 30 years of age when John baptised him in the muddy waters of the Jordan river. The experience seemed to have moved him deeply, because he withdrew to the lonely hills above the Dead Sea. It was here, alone in the wilderness, after forty days and forty nights of fasting and praying, Jesus was tempted by the devil.

His public life as a religious leader began almost immediately, and he started preaching the Kingdom of God in Galilee, in the region of Capernaum. He travelled alone, going from place to place and preaching in the local synagogues. The Kingdom of God, Jesus said, was the Kingdom of the pure in heart. God was the Father of all, they were His Children. Therefore everyone should love God and love one another. If they were truly sorry for their sins and placed their trust in God, and believed in His mercy, they would be forgiven. As Jesus' fame spread, (due to his miraculous healing power), many people came to him with their illnesses, and he healed them. All were amazed at his teaching, because his message had authority. He became so popular that men, women and children followed him everywhere. One day, as Jesus stood by the Lake of Gennesaret (The Sea of Galilee), a large number of people crowded around to hear him teach.

He asked some nearby fishermen, who were washing their nets, to row him out into deeper water and let down the nets for a catch. This suggestion made little sense to Simon Peter, since he had fished all night and caught nothing. But, he did what Jesus asked of him. Incredibly, in a few seconds of lowering down the nets, so many fish were trapped in the net that it began to break. Simon Peter signalled his fishing partners in the other boat on the shore for help. They came quickly and brought up so many fish that both of the boats were filled. When they all reached the shore, Simon Peter fell at Jesus' feet, saying he was a sinner. Astonished at the large catch of fish, Simon Peter and his partners, James and John left their boats and fish to follow Jesus, who promised to make them *fishers of men.*

According to the Gospel of Luke, they were the first of Jesus' disciples to be called. Some people however refused to believe in the miracles that Jesus performed, noticeably his home-town of Nazareth when he returned there. The people just thought that he was Jesus the son of Joseph the carpenter. One Sabbath day, he went into the synagogue, and when it came for his turn to read a portion of Scripture, Jesus read aloud a passage from the Book of Isaiah.

> *"The Spirit of the LORD is on me because He has*
> *anointed me to preach good news to the poor.*
> *He has sent me to proclaim freedom for the prisoners*
> *and recovery of sight to the blind,*
> *to release the oppressed,*
> *To proclaim the year of the LORD'S favour."*
> (ISAIAH 61:1-2)

Rolling up the scroll and turning to the people listening, Jesus said:

"Today this Scripture has been fulfiled in your hearing." (LUKE 4:21).

They were bewildered. They had seen Jesus grow into manhood, just an ordinary human being, just like themselves. And here, right now, he was trying to convince them that he was in fact the LORD'S Anointed One!

Why didn't Jesus prove it with miracles if he wanted them to believe? But, Jesus hinted that the people living in Nazareth would not see any miracles because of their lack of faith. That was too much. They rose up in anger and took him to the brow of a hill above the village to throw him over a cliff, but somehow he walked right through the crowd and went on his way.

He returned to Capernaum and taught in the synagogue there on the Sabbath days. People were amazed at Jesus' teachings. They were used to hearing the Scribes and the Pharisees discuss the fine points of the Laws of Moses. The Scribes were experts in the Law, and served as teachers, explaining the Law to the people. The most learned ones were called Doctors of the Law, to indicate that they were Scribes of great knowledge and authority. Many Scribes belonged to a strict religious sect called the Pharisees. Its members tried to live pure lives under the Law, and to set an example for others to follow. The Scribes and the Pharisees enjoyed talking about the meaning of words, and they liked to compare different passages in the Scriptures.

For the simple village folk such discussions were very dry and difficult to understand. Much of Palestine in Jesus' day was an illiterate society, but Jesus spoke to them in the everyday language of the people using *'Parables'* (stories).

7

He talked about the simple laws of the Heavenly Father. Everybody likes a story, and stories are easier to remember than concepts or logical outlines. Jesus spoke in terms that would hold the interest of a society of mainly farmers and fishermen. He explained what he meant by using his natural surroundings; Jesus used stories about fishermen, farmers, lost sheep, wayward sons, a Sower of seeds, and many other familiar things that were part of their daily lives. Even the children could understand him. There was even something about his manner of speaking, that was different, too. He spoke as one who had higher authority. His disciples rapidly increased in number. To become a disciple a man had to sacrifice all that was his. He had to leave home and family, give up all his possessions, and follow Jesus with no thought of his earthly needs. From then one, he had no home. He led a wandering existence, following Jesus from place to place. Sometimes, the disciples stayed in the homes of friends. More often they slept under the olive and sycamore trees, wrapped in their woollen cloaks. They ate what was given to them, usually unleavened bread, dates, raisins, honey and sometimes cheese.

Whenever they were near a lake they would eat fish, if they had time to catch them. Jesus often used his disciples as stewards, to handle the great crowds that came to hear him teach. People came from Jerusalem and from all parts of Judea, and from the seacoast of Tyre and Sidon, and from the region beyond the Jordan. One day, seeing the great multitudes that followed him, Jesus led them up onto a mountainside. Together with his disciples he sat down and spoke to them, saying:

*"Blessed are the poor in spirit,
for theirs is the Kingdom of Heaven.
Blessed are those who mourn, for they will be comforted.
Blessed are the meek, for they will inherit the earth.
Blessed are those who hunger and thirst for righteousness,
for they will be filled.
Blessed are the merciful, for they will be shown mercy.
Blessed are the pure in heart, for they will see God.
Blessed are the peacemakers, for they will be called sons of God.
Blessed are you when people insult you, persecute you and falsely
say all kinds of evil against you because of me. Rejoice and be glad,
because great is your reward in Heaven, for in the same way they
persecuted the Prophets who were before you.
Blessed are those who are persecuted because of righteousness, for
theirs is the Kingdom of Heaven.* (MATTHEW 5:3-12)*

Jesus said he had not come to set aside their religion and start another. He had not come to destroy the sacred writings of the Law and the prophets of old. He had come, rather, to fulfil the Law and the Prophets and to bring them into perfection. The people listening had been taught the ancient saying: *"An eye for an eye, and a tooth for a tooth."* But Jesus told them vengeance was wrong. He told them not to resist the wrongful acts of others. If someone struck them on the right cheek, they were to turn the other also. They had been taught: *"Thou shalt love thy neighbour, and hate their enemy. "* But, Jesus said they should not hate anyone. He told them to love their enemies, and to repay evil with good. He told them not to store up treasures on earth, but rather to store up treasures in heaven, where rust or moth cannot destroy or thieves cannot steal or break into, *"For where your treasure is, there your heart will be also."* (MATTHEW 6:21).

No man could serve two masters. He had to make a choice between material things on earth and the Kingdom of Heaven. Jesus told them: *"You cannot serve both God and money"* (v 24). Jesus told them to be merciful. Judge no-one, and you shall not be judged. Condemn not, and you shall not be condemned. Forgive, and you shall be forgiven. Give, and you shall be given in return in good measure. All things that you would like to have others do unto you, do you also unto them. Jesus told them to put their trust in God, and have faith:

"Ask, and it will be given you; seek and you will find; knock and the door will be opened to you. For everyone who asks receives; he who seeks finds; and to him who knocks, the door will be opened." (7:7)

The sermon Jesus made on the mountain summed up much that he had been teaching in the synagogues. Jesus revealed the true intent of the Old Testament Law, rather than its legalistic interpretations in simplest terms. But many people were disappointed and astonished at his teachings. They had come to find the leader God had promised them, a king who would lead them against the Romans. Instead, Jesus had spoken against hate and vengeance.

Out of his large group of disciples, Jesus chose twelve to be his special helpers. These he called apostles. They were Simon Peter; Andrew; James and his brother John; Philip; Bartholomew; who was also known as Nathaniel; Thomas; James, son of Alpheus, who was called James "the less" because he was much younger than the other James; Matthew the Publican, the word publican meaning a public official who collected Roman taxes; Simon the Zealot; Jude, also known as Thaddeus; and Judas Iscariot. They were all simple men of great faith. All were Galileans, except for Judas Iscariot, who was from Judea. He probably had some education, for he was chosen as treasurer of the group.

Simon Peter, an impulsive, outspoken man who believed in action, usually acted as their leader. One day Jesus asked his disciples who people said he was. They replied that some thought he was John the Baptiser, some Elijah, or one of the Prophets. *"But what about you?"*, Jesus asked. *"Who do you say I am?"* Simon Peter answered him. *"You are the Christ, the Son of the Living God."* ('**Christ**' was a Greek word that meant the *Messiah, the Anointed One*).

Jesus replied, *"Blessed are you, Simon son of Jonah, for this was not revealed to you by man, but my Father in heaven. And I tell you that you are Peter, and on this rock I will build my church and the gates of Hades (hell) will not overcome it."* (Matthew 16:18)

He began to prepare them for what was to come, by foretelling his death in Jerusalem, and told them he would rise to life again on the third day. His disciples heard him, but did not understand.

Simon Peter who had won high praise from Jesus for discerning his true identity began rebuking Jesus, and told him that his death would never happen. Jesus turned and said to Peter, *"Get behind me Satan! You are a stumbling-block to me; you do not have in mind the things of God, but the things of men."*

When Jesus had trained the apostles, he sent them out in two's to preach the Kingdom of God. They took nothing with them, trusting God would provide for their needs. Their mission did not last long, but it gave them experience. They returned to Jesus filled with wonder and amazement at the miracles they had been able to perform. However, Jesus reminded them frequently of the importance of faith. He emphasised, if they had faith, all things would be possible for them. They could say to this mountain, move, and it would move. The test of faith proved a difficult one for Jesus' apostles, and even Simon Peter's faith failed him more than once on numerous occasions. It failed him one night as he and the rest of the disciples were rowing across the Sea of Galilee. Suddenly, in the dim starlight, they saw the figure of a man walking toward them across the water. The frightened disciples believing it to be a ghost cried out in fear. But Jesus identified himself and told them not to be afraid. Peter shouted back: *"LORD, if it is you, tell me to come to you on the water."* Jesus replied, *'Come."* Climbing out of the boat, Simon Peter began walking on top of the water. But when he felt the wind and saw the water moving under his feet, he became frightened and began to sink crying out: *"LORD, save me!"* Jesus reached out and caught his hand and helped him climb back into the boat replying: *'You of little faith, why did you doubt?'*

Performed miracles usually removed those who doubted, but not always. Some of the miracles done by Jesus actually created doubt in the minds of the people, and also caused many of his early followers to turn away from him.

In the village of Cana, he healed the dying son of a Roman officer. Later, he cured the servant of another Roman in

Capernaum. He also cured the daughter of a Canaanite woman. None of these people believed in the true God and they were therefore looked down upon by the Jews. The Romans, were the much hated enemy of the Jewish people, and any Jew who helped a Roman was surely a traitor to his people. The Jews were proud of being the *'Chosen People of God'*, but Jesus asked them to believe all men were God's children. To the proud chosen Jewish race, it was implying that they were no better than others. To them it seemed like an insult that struck at the very heart of their pride as a people. The Pharisees were quick to point this out. They were angered by the way Jesus and his disciples calmly disregarded many of the rules which they themselves held sacred. For example, the Sabbath day (traditionally Saturday for Jews), was regarded by the Pharisees as Holy, a day of worship and rest but, Jesus had performed many miracles on a Sabbath day.

Over the centuries, the Pharisees had worked out a complicated set of rules based on their interpretation of the Laws of Moses. The Pharisees had begun to make these rules because they were alarmed at the way Jews were mingling with other peoples who did not believe in the true God. These non-believers, called pagans, worshiped many false gods and goddesses. They looked down upon the Jews, because the Jews worshiped only one God. But where Jews and pagans lived side by side, they became friendly. Many Jews became careless about their religion and some even married pagan women, giving up their own Jewish religion.

In order to keep the Jews together as a people and to

strengthen their faith, the Pharisees started to make rules. One of these rules forbid Jews from mingling with pagans. Other rules were made to help uneducated Jews live good religious lives under the Laws of Moses. The trouble was that the Pharisees continued making rules year after year, which upset the majority of Jews who began to complain, for their religious duties had become a burden to them and took too much of their time.

Another Jewish sect, called the Sadducees, were also strongly opposed to the Pharisees and their rules. The Sadducees were well-established Jews who thought more of their pride and comfort than they did of their religion. They were more than willing to associate with pagans, especially when they could profit by it, and refused to have anything to do with the rules of the Pharisees. Jesus had nothing in common with the Sadducees. He was closer to the Pharisees in his thinking; for he too believed the Law was sacred. When Jesus criticised the Pharisees, as often as he did, it was because he felt that they followed the letter rather than the spirit of the Law. For this reason, Jesus ignored many of the rules of the Pharisees. They fasted regularly on Mondays and Thursday's. Jesus did not. The Pharisees were shocked, when they saw Jesus dining in the homes of tax collectors, who were regarded as sinners, and even more so, when he chose Matthew, as an apostle. To them they believed that such people were unclean, and advised all good Jews should avoid even the slightest contact with them. The most honoured of all the rules of the Pharisees had to do with the keeping of the Sabbath. No one was allowed to work on the Sabbath, or even pluck fruit from a tree - it was strictly forbidden. Naturally, the Pharisees were deeply upset when they heard that the disciples of Jesus had picked grain heads and eaten the kernels on the Sabbath day, as they walked through the fields. To make things worse, Jesus healed a number of people on the Sabbath. On one of his early visits to Jerusalem, he took some mud and made a clay paste and used it to on the eyes of a blind man to restore his sight. This his did on a Sabbath, and making clay on this day was strictly forbidden. To the Pharisees this proved that Jesus was a sinner. Any man who made clay on the Sabbath, could not have been sent by God.

From that time on, they had Jesus constantly watched, hoping to find something they could use against him. Jesus felt that the Jews did not really understand the full meaning of the Second Commandment, that you should love your neighbour as yourself. A Pharisee asked Jesus: *"And who is my neighbour?"* Instead of answering him directly Jesus told him a short story, a parable, to illustrate his point. It was common in those days for people to tell parables when they were trying to explain something, and Jesus was particularly good at it. Jesus said, there once was a man, who was attacked by thieves and left half dead by the side of the road. A priest came that way and passed by the wounded man. Next came a Levite, who assisted the priests in the Temple. He too, saw the man and passed him by. Then came a Samaritan from the province of Samaria. He took pity on the man, went to him with oil and wine and nursed him by bandaging his wounds. Jesus then asked: *"Which of these three, do you think proved a good neighbour by showing mercy to the man who fell into the robbers hands?"* The question was not an easy one. Jesus had added a twist by making the one who showed love a Samaritan - a racial minority despised in Israel; for Jews looked upon Samaritans as being even lower than animals. How could a Samaritan be a neighbour? But the Pharisee saw the point and answered, *"the one who showed mercy on him."* Jesus told him, *'Go and do like wise.'*

In this story, Jesus had contrasted mere religious beliefs with true love. According to Old Testament Law, a priest who touched a dead body made himself ceremonially impure (LEVITICUS 21:1-4). Therefore, the Priest and religious Levite decided not to get involved. The Pharisee and the listening audience might have expected the third character to be a Jewish layperson. But Jesus captured their attention by making the one who showed love a Samaritan, who were hated by the Jews in Israel.

Jesus preached mainly in Judea, in the region around Jerusalem, during the last months of his life. He was in the city in October for the *Feast of Tabernacles*, and again in December for the *Ceremony of Dedication*. On both occasions he carried out his religious duties as one of the Jewish faith. The teachings of Jesus were based on the Holy Scriptures, and on his Jewish faith. He frequently referred to the Scriptures when he spoke to the people. What he had to say about the *"golden rule"* and love was based on the teachings of Jewish Rabbi's, like Hillel and on passages in the Scriptures. Unfortunately, these passages were overlooked by many Jews in their strong desire to set themselves apart as the Chosen People.

One day, when Jesus was in Judea, a disciple asked him how to pray. Jesus taught him this prayer:

"Our Father who art in Heaven, Hallowed be Your name. Thy kingdom come, Thy will be done, on earth as it is in heaven. Give us this day our daily bread, And forgive us our debts, as we also forgive our debtors; And lead us not into temptation, but deliver us from the evil one."
(MATTHEW 6:9-13).

Jesus described himself in many ways. He said:
"I am the bread of life. He who comes to me will never go hungry, and he who believes in me will never be thirsty."
(JOHN 6:35).
At another time he said, *"I am the light of the world. Whoever follows me, will never walk in darkness, but will have the light of life."* (JOHN 8:12).
The Jews knew what **"the light"** meant. It was one of the phrases used in the Scriptures to describe the *Messiah*. The Jews argued among themselves about the sayings Jesus spoke. Some of them said, *"He has a demon."* Others said, *"Can a demon open the eyes of the blind?"* One day they found Jesus walking in the Temple and demanded a straight answer: *"If you are the Christ, tell us plainly."* Jesus answered them, *"I told you, and you do not believe. The works (miracles), that I do in my Father's name, they bear witness to me…."*
(JOHN 14:10-11).

To the Jews this was blasphemy, a sin against God. They tried to arrest him, but he quietly slipped away from their grasp to the land beyond the Jordan. He later returned again to Judea, when he heard that his friend, Lazarus lay ill in Bethany. That village was only an hour's walking distance from Jerusalem. Jesus often stayed there as a guest in the home of Lazarus and his sisters, who he loved. By the time Jesus and his disciples arrived, Lazarus was dead, and had been in his grave four days. Jesus had the stone rolled away from the entrance of the grave and brought the dead man back to life, after calling his name. It was one of his last miracles, and it caused so much excitement in Jerusalem, that the chief priests and Pharisees met to search for a way to put Jesus to death.

Many doubted that he would dare to appear for the Passover. The Passover celebrated the great escape of the Jews from slavery in Egypt. (EXODUS 12). But the chief priests and Pharisees watched out for Jesus, thinking he might slip quietly into the city. Then on Sunday, before the Passover they were amazed to see him ride boldly on a donkey into the city, leading a great multitude of people who laid down their robes, and palm and olive branches in front of him shouting:

"Blessed be the King, who comes in the name of the LORD! Peace in heaven, and glory in the highest!"

During the days that followed, Jesus taught daily in the Temple. The Pharisees feared that this would cause trouble with the Romans, but they dared not arrest him, for he had won many supporters. Instead, they tried to trap him with various questions.

"Tell us then, what is your opinion? Is it right to pay taxes to Caesar", they asked. Jesus knew he would lose the respect of many Jews if he approved the hated Roman tax. But if he said the tax was unlawful, he would be reported to the Roman authorities, who would arrest and imprison him. Jesus asked them whose image do you see on the coin used for paying the

tax. *"Caesar's"*, they answered. Jesus continued, *"Then give to Caesar what is Caesar's, and to God what is God's."* (MATTHEW 22: 15-22).

They plied him with other questions, too, but could not find fault with his answers. During all this time, Judas Iscariot, one of the twelve apostles, went secretly to the chief priests and offered to lead them to Jesus at a time when people were not about, so that he could be arrested quietly. The chief priests were delighted, and agreed to pay Judas Iscariot, thirty pieces of silver. At sundown, on the Thursday before Passover, Jesus and his disciples met in a large upper-room of a house in the city and shared the feast of the unleavened bread. Why the feast was eaten on the Thursday instead of Friday is not known. But there is a tradition that the Galileans and some others observed the feast a day early when Passover occurred on the Sabbath.

Jesus took bread, broke it, and gave it to his disciples, saying: *"Take and eat, this is my body."* Then he offered then wine in a cup, saying, *"Drink from it, all of you. This is my blood of the covenant, which is poured out for you for many for the forgiveness of sins."* (MATTHEW 26:17-30).

Once again Jesus foretold his death, and also said one of his apostles, would betray him. He promised that god would send them a Comforter, the Holy Spirit. After singing a hymn, they left the city and went to an olive grove called *Gethsemane* on the 'Mount of Olives'. They had previously spent other nights there. Judas Iscariot knew the place also. He arrived during the night with a large party of temple servants and soldiers, all carrying swords and clubs. Judas had arranged with the chief priests and elders, to betray Jesus with a single kiss. They arrested Jesus and took him to Caiaphas, the high priest's house. There the priests and teachers of the Law assembled a hearing and brought many witnesses against him. Finally the high priest stood up and asked Jesus: *"I charge you under oath by the Living God: Tell us if you are the Christ, the Son of God?"* Jesus answered, *"Yes it as you say. But I say to all of you: In the future you will see the Son of Man, sitting at the right hand of the Mighty One and coming on the clouds of Heaven."* The high priest tore his clothes and said to the others, *"He has spoken blasphemy! What do you think?"* (MATTHEW 26: 47-68). All those assembled agreed that Jesus was guilty, and that he should die. They decided to take him to Pontius Pilate, the Roman governor of Judea, who alone had the power to order the death penalty. When, Judas Iscariot heard that Jesus had been condemned to death by the council of elders, he had a change of heart. He tried to return the thirty pieces of silver, but the priests refused to touch it. In despair and remorse, Judas threw away the blood money into the temple and went out and hanged himself.

The chief priests brought Jesus to Pontius Pilate and told him: *"We found this man perverting our nation, and forbidding to give tribute to Caesar, and saying, he himself is Christ a king."* Pilate questioned him, and when he learned that Jesus was from Galilee he sent him to King Herod, the ruler of Galilee, who was also in the city at that time. Before this day both Pilate and Herod were enemies, but Jesus' trial made them friends. Meanwhile, Herod made fun of Jesus and sent him back to Pilate, dressed in a robe so that he looked like a king.

JESUS' DEATH BY CRUCIFIXION

There was a tradition around the period of A.D 29, that the Roman governor should release a prisoner to the people at the time of the Passover. Pilate asked, *"Which of the two, do you want me to release to you, Barabbas or Jesus, who is called Christ?"* Barabbas, was a well-known robber and insurrectionist, but the priests instructed the people call his name. So they cried for the release of Barabbas, and demanded that Jesus be crucified. Pilate who could not find any crime against Jesus, wanted to release him, but the people said: *"If you release this man, you are not Caesar's friend; everyone who makes himself a king sets himself against Caesar."*

The argument disturbed Pilate, who especially did not want to do anything which might lead to mis-understanding between himself and Caesar. It could be a difficult charge to answer, so Pilate, asked, *"Shall I crucify your king?"* The chief priests replied, *"We have no king but Caesar."*

Pilate eventually surrendered to their demands. He had Jesus turned over to the soldiers to be crucified. The soldiers flogged Jesus with leather whips, which carried sharp, razor-like, ball-bearings on the end of the thongs. These whips were purposely made to expose (strip), a man's skin to reveal flesh and bone. Dressing Jesus up, by putting a purple robe on him, and twisting a crown of thorns on his head, the soldier's then began to strike Jesus' body with their fists and rods. They even plucked his beard , spat at him and mocked him, shouting and falling on their knees: *"Hail, king of the Jews!"*, they shouted to him, paying homage to him. When they had finished mocking Jesus, the soldiers replaced the purple robe with his own clothes and led him beyond the walls of the city to a hill called *Golgotha*, which means ***"the place of the skull"***.

There, Jesus of Nazareth was crucified on a Cross between two robbers. Many of the chief priests and the teachers of the Law passed by the Cross, taunting him, as he hung there nailed and naked to the Cross, (nails which were pounded through his wrist and heel bones). *"If you are the Son of God, come down from the Cross and save yourself!"*, they shouted. Others said, *"He saved many others; let him save himself, if he is the Christ of God, the Chosen One!"*

At the sixth hour, darkness came over the whole land, and, about the ninth hour Jesus cried in a loud voice: **"ELOI, ELOI, lama sabachtani?"** - which means, *"My God, My God, Why have You Forsaken me?"*

One man standing nearby ran and filled a sponge with vinegar, and placing it on a stick, gave Jesus a drink. A few minutes later, Jesus cried out in a loud voice, *"It is finished!"*, and breathed his last words saying, *"Father, into Your hands I commit my spirit."*

The BURIAL and RESURRECTION of JESUS

Jesus of Nazareth, lived and died a Jew. Like the ancient Hebrew teachers, he urged all men, women and children to love the God of the whole Universe and to love their fellow man (neighbour), with the same God-like love. He left no writings of his own, and his public ministry was short, possibly not as long as two years or so. Yet, Jesus' influence on world history might not have had such a great impact if **HIS** story had not ended by death on the Cross at Calvary Hill.

Also, Jesus' story does not end with his crucifixion and neither does the "GOSPEL of JESUS CHRIST." Jesus of Nazareth, died on a Friday, and to speed the death of those victims crucified on Fridays, so that they could be buried before the Sabbath, their legs were usually broken. But, Jesus was found to be dead already, so they did not break his legs. Rather, to make sure he was certified dead, one of the soldiers standing nearby thrust his spear into the side of Jesus.

On Preparation Day (the day before the Sabbath), one Joseph of Arimathea, a prominent member of the council received permission from Pontius Pilate, to take the body of Jesus away for burial. With, Nicodemus and the help of friends, he placed Jesus' crucified body, wrapped in some linen cloth, in a new sepulcher in a nearby garden. The grave was really a cave hollowed out of a rock in the side of a hill. Over the entrance, they had rolled into place a huge stone. The following day (Sabbath Day), nothing more was done. Early, Sunday morning, Mary Magdalene, out of whom Jesus had driven seven demons, and other followers of Jesus brought sweet spices to anoint Jesus' body, but they found the stone rolled away and the tomb empty. Bewildered and frightened, the others ran leaving Mary behind weeping. While she was crying by the side of the tomb, Jesus suddenly appeared before her. That same evening in Jerusalem, Jesus appeared before a number of disciples gathered together in a locked room. The disciples were terrified, for they thought Jesus was a ghost.But, Jesus reassured them all that he was not a spirit, by saying:

"Why are you troubled? See my hands and my feet, that it is I, myself; handle me, and see; for a spirit has no flesh or bones as you see that I have."

Doubting, they still stared at him.

Jesus then asked, *"Have you anything here to eat?"*

They gave him a piece of broiled fish and a honeycomb. He took and ate these before them.

The Gospel of John, also mentions Jesus appearing in various other places after his resurrection from the dead, to his disciples and other people, performing many miracles. He met with the apostles in the mountains of Galilee and instructed them to teach and witness to all nations, *"baptising them in the name of the Father, and of the Son, and of the Holy Spirit, teaching them to obey everything he had taught them, because he would be them always, to the very end of age."*

(MATTHEW 28: 18-20)

In the Gospel story, as told by Luke (an Historian, Doctor and gifted writer), found in the King James version of the Holy Bible, it ends with these lines:

"And it came to pass, while he (Jesus) blessed them, he was parted from them, and carried up into Heaven. And they worshiped him, and returned to Jerusalem with great joy: And where continually in the Temple, praising and blessing God. Amen."

This, then, is the Gospel of Jesus Christ. His followers were so convinced that Jesus had risen from the dead and had ascended into Heaven, that his resurrection became the very focus of their faith. Jesus of Nazareth had risen from the dead.

He had conquered death's penalty. He was therefore truly the Son of God, the long-promised *Messiah* of the ancient prophets.

CHRISTIANITY, IS IT TRUE?

Christianity is unique among the religions of the world. It is based on the conviction that its founder Jesus Christ of Nazareth, rose from the dead on the first Easter day. The resurrection is the cornerstone on which the whole of Christianity, both in its corporate and individual aspects, is built. If it is false, the entire edifice collapses. If it is true, the consequences for our world and for individual lives are immense.

The whole key to Christianity is undoubtedly focused, on the resurrection of Jesus from the grave. We do not know of anyone else in all history, who has had this experience or caused so much commotion. It is only expected that a supernatural person should come to, and, leave the earth in a supernatural way. Jesus' birth was natural, but his resurrection was supernatural. His miraculous conception and resurrection do not prove his deity, but they are congruous with it. There are many people to this very day, who maintain their personal view, and would have us believe that Jesus did not really die on the Cross, but only fainted. The so-called *"Swoon"* or *"fake"* theory. Some people have said and even written books, mentioning Jesus was even *"swapped"*, by his disciples. That another person looking exactly like Jesus replaced him; some people even think that Judas Iscariot replaced Jesus.

All these so-called theories concerning the death of Jesus of Nazareth, simply bristle with problems. They are all thoroughly perverse. The evidence found in the Holy Bible, entirely contradicts them. For example, Pontius Pilate, was convinced by the assurance of a Centurion's testimony that Jesus was dead, he allowed Joseph of Arimathea permission to remove the body from the Cross. The Roman centurion was certain of Jesus' death because he must have been present with many other guards when *"one of the soldiers pierced his side with a spear, and at once there came out blood and water."* The **"Blood and Water"**, from the spear thrust into Jesus' side, is proof positive that he was already dead. Had Jesus been alive still when the spear pierced his side, strong spurts of blood would have emerged with every heartbeat.

Are we seriously to believe that Jesus could have been faking his own death? After, all the rigours, pains of the trial, mockery, flogging, severe punishment and crucifixion, could he really survive thirty-six hours in a strong sealed sepulchre, with neither warmth nor food or medical care, and Roman soldiers posted to guard the tomb? And, after this, weak, sickly and hungry could appear to his disciples in such a way as to give them the impression that he had vanquished death? That, he could go on to claim he had died and then risen, could send them into all the world and promise to be with them unto the end of time? That he could live somewhere in hiding for forty days, making occasional surprise appearances, and then finally disappears without any explanation? Such credulity I would have to say, is more incredible than the disciple, Thomas' unbelief.

God has revealed Himself to all mankind through the Holy Bible. The Holy Bible, consists of both the Old and the New

Testaments, but, every word written down was inspired by God's Spirit through human authors, so that the Holy Bible as originally given is in its entirety the Word of God, without fault or error and fully reliable in truth, fact, and doctrine. The Holy Bible, (particularly the New testament), tells us about the birth, life, and death and resurrection of Jesus Christ, and the life and growth of the Christian church in the first-century. God sent the Word into this world as Jesus Christ (JOHN 1: 1-14).

For thirty-three and a half years, Jesus obeyed and served his father by speaking the Father's heavenly words. Jesus' whole life here on earth was in total obedience to his Father's love for all humanity. Jesus' life 2,000 years ago in Palestine, explained to all men and women, what it really means to love God, to seek God, to serve God, and to be like God in thought, word or deed. For Jesus, loved his Father with all his heart, soul, mind, and with all hi strength. He also loved his fellow neighbour more than himself because he gave his very own life for all - his neighbour, his enemy and the entire population of the world.

(JOHN 3:16)
This verse has probably been memorised more than any other in the Holy Bible. In a few words (20) it tells the story of salvation: God's love for the world, God's gift of his Son, and the opportunity for anyone who believes in Jesus Christ, His Son to be saved. It is the whole Gospel of Jesus Christ in a nutshell.

Who, then, is Jesus? And why is history, really **HIS story**? Jesus is God, Man, Creator, High Priest and the Sacrificial Lamb for all mankind's sin. More importantly, Jesus was like all other humans and yet different from every one. He was tested like any human, and **yet he was the only person ever born who lived his entire life without ever committing a sin.** No other human in all history has been able to avoid sin. *"For all have sinned and fallen short of the glory of God"* (ROMANS 3:23).

This is what makes Jesus Christ of Nazareth so unique, so special. Jesus was fully God and fully Man. Jesus Christ never sinned. His death on the Cross paid humanity's debt of sin. Jesus Christ is our Saviour, the only Saviour and King of all kings and Lord of all lords, because He was - and still is - God.

Jesus is the perfect role model for the entire human race, in living and in suffering. He is our perfect example for loving and trusting in God. He gave us all the free opportunity of redemption, healing, deliverance, salvation and everlasting life. *"At the Name of Jesus every knee should bow ... and every tongue confess that Jesus Christ is LORD."*
(PHILIPPIANS 2:10-11)

Jesus was a man born in an obscure village, the child of a young Jewish peasant woman. He grew up in still another village, where he worked in a carpenter's shop until he was 30. For the next three years he was an itinerant preacher. He never wrote a book. He never held an office. He never had a family or owned a house. He didn't go to University or College. He never travelled more than 200 miles from the place where he was born. He did none of the things one usually associates with greatness. When he was 33, the tide of public opinion turned against him. His best friends (the disciples) ran away. He was betrayed by one of his own disciples kisses, turned over to his enemies and went through the humiliating mockery of a trial. He was nailed to the Cross between two thieves. When he was dying, his executioners played a lottery gambling game, for his clothing which was the only property he had on earth. When he was pierced in his side by a Roman soldier's spear and pronounced dead, he was then laid in a borrowed grave, through the kindness of a friend.

Now, nineteen centuries have come and gone and today Jesus Christ of Nazareth *is* the central figure of the human race and the leader of mankind's progress. All the armies that ever marched, all the navies that ever sailed, all the parliaments that ever sat, all the kings who ever reigned, put together, have not affected the life of man on earth as much as Jesus Christ has done.

Is He *your* Saviour? Is He Lord of *your* life today? Is He directing your footsteps? If He is not, I ask you now to take a look for yourself at some of the Scriptures found in the New Testament of the Holy Bible, confirming, that God's way of Salvation for all mankind is only through His Son Jesus Christ.

GOD'S WAY OF SALVATION FOR ALL MANKIND
"Salvation is found in no-one else, for there is no other name under heaven given to men by which we must be saved."
(ACTS 4:12)

"Christ Jesus came into the world to save sinners."
(1 TIMOTHY 1:15)

*"God wants all men/women to be saved
and to come to the knowledge of truth."*
(1 TIMOTHY 2:4)

*"We testify that the Father has sent His Son
to be the Saviour of the world."*
(1 JOHN 4:14)

*"What must I do to be saved?....
Believe in the Lord Jesus Christ, and you will be saved."*
(ACTS 16:30-31)

*"If we confess our sins, He is faithful and just to forgive us
our sins and purify us from all unrighteousness."*
(1 JOHN 1: 9)

*"If you confess with your mouth, "Jesus is Lord", and
believe in your heart that God raised Him from the dead,
you will be saved. For it is with your heart you believe and
are justified, and it is with your mouth that you confess
and are saved. Everyone who calls on the name of the Lord
will be saved."*
(ROMANS 10: 9-10,13)

*"In reply Jesus declared, 'I tell you the truth, no-one can
see the Kingdom of God unless he is Born Again........'
You must be Born Again."*
(JOHN 3: verses 3 and 7)

THE BIBLE SAYS THERE IS ONLY ONE WAY TO HEAVEN

Jesus said, *"I am the Way, the Truth, and the Life: no man cometh unto the Father, but by me."* (JOHN 14:6)

Nobody Except Jesus Christ Can Save Your Soul

1. Admit you are a sinner in need of a Saviour.
2. Be willing to turn from your sin **(repent)**.
3. Believe that Jesus Christ died for you personally, was buried and rose from the dead on the third day.
4. Through a simple sincere prayer, invite Jesus into your life to become your Lord and personal Saviour.

WHAT TO PRAY

"Dear Lord Jesus, I come to you right now a sinner in need of a Saviour. I ask you to forgive me of all my sins, and wash me in Your precious blood. I accept Christ's sacrifice as perfect and complete. I ask Jesus Christ to come into my life, to change my life and to be my very best friend. I place my trust in Him alone for my salvation. Thank You for giving me eternal life, and thank you for writing my name in the Lamb's Book of Life. I believe now, I am Born Again, a brand new creation in Christ in God, and I ask You Lord Jesus, that Your Holy Spirit will fill me now with Your love, from the crown of my head to the soles of my feet, in Jesus' magnificent name!" - AMEN.

Did you pray this prayer and accept Jesus Christ into your heart as your own personal Saviour?

If your answer was yes, then I congratulate you my friend, for this is just the beginning of a wonderful brand new life with Jesus Christ. Now:

1) You must read your Holy Bible everyday to get to know Christ better.

2) Pray to God everyday (in your own words).

3) Be water-baptised as soon as possible, worship, fellowship, and serve with other Christians in a church where Christ is preached and the Holy Bible is the final authority.

4) You must tell others about Jesus Christ.

ON THE ROAD WITH
APOSTLE PAUL

INTRODUCTION

My aim in writing this book is to investigate and give a detailed account of the life of Saul (Apostle Paul) of Tarsus to his death, from A.D. 35-64.

Never has there been a man in all the earth whose life changed quickly and dramatically, as Paul's did. Paul (formerly called Saul) made his first appearance in Acts (8:1), assisting at the brutal stoning of Stephen. Later he led a gang of persecutors on a violent campaign against Christian believers. But, then came a miraculous turnabout on the road to Damascus (9:1-19).

Paul spearheaded the campaign to grant Gentiles full acceptance without subjecting them to Jewish Law. He had himself been liberated from bondage to confining laws, and he insisted on a life based on God's free forgiveness, not legalism.

During his journeys, Paul wrote half the New Testament books, and in them he laid the groundwork for much of Christian theology. All the while he carried on a courageous career despite jailing's, beatings and riots. He was perhaps the most thoroughly converted man who ever lived. So let us now look at Paul's life, by taking a walk with me, "on the road with Apostle Paul".....

On the Road With Apostle Paul

There was a one man who had more to do with the future of the Christian church than even the apostles themselves. His name was Paul, or Saul in Hebrew. He was the greatest of all Christian missionaries. Much more is known about Paul than about other leaders of the early church, for he wrote or dictated long letters of instruction and encouragement to various missions he had established. These letters were called epistles. A number of them were preserved and published. In addition, most of the Acts of the Apostles, the fifth book of the New Testament, deals with Paul and his teachings. Taken together, his epistles, and the chapters of the book of Acts devoted to him almost one half of the New Testament.

One of the most amazing things about Paul was that he first came to the attention of the brethren in Jerusalem as a dangerous enemy of the church. He was first mentioned in Acts as one of those present during the stoning of Stephen: "Meanwhile, the witnesses laid their clothes at the feet of a young man named Saul". (Acts 7:58b) He was one of the angry mob crying for the blood of Stephen, and he guarded the cloaks of the executioners while they were casting their stones. Paul was the kind of man who had to live by his faith. He was a Pharisee, well-educated in the Law, proud of his rich Jewish heritage, and deeply loved the God of Israel. Anyone who mocked or offended God was guilty of blasphemy and deserved to be punished. There was no doubt in Paul's mind that Stephen was guilty. Paul hated him for it, and eagerly joined with those whom he believed to be carrying out the

Lord's punishment.

According to tradition, Paul was short, broad-shouldered, with a slightly hooked nose and heavy brows that almost came together. He was born a few years after the birth of Jesus, in the Greek city of Tarsus, the capital of Cilicia, another Roman province. Somehow his family had obtained Roman citizenship, which gave them certain rights and privileges most people in the provinces did not have.

"WHO ARE YOU LORD?"
His father taught him the trade of a tentmaker. When Paul was fifteen he went to study religion under the famous religious teachers of the Temple, for it was his ambition to become a recognised expert in the Law. He studied the Bible in Hebrew, Greek, and Aramaic under the most famous Pharisee teacher in the Holy City, Gamiliel the Elder. How long Paul studied in Jerusalem is not known. But he was in Jerusalem when Stephen was stoned to death, and approximately thirty years old.

Such was Paul's hatred for the followers of Jesus that he led a campaign of terror against them, hunting down the Christians in every backstreet of the city, and even in the nearby villages. Not content with that, he went to the high priest and asked for letters to the synagogues of Damascus. He wanted authority to arrest the Christians there and bring them back to Jerusalem for trial and punishment. The high priest gave him letters and also an armed escort to guard the prisoners on the way back. Paul and his escort set out at once. They followed the ancient caravan trail up through Palestine and across the steppes for eight days. They were nearing Damascus when something happened to Paul. He may have had a vision, or some great emotional experience. Whatever it was, Paul's description of it is the same as that found in the Book of Acts.

According to Paul, he and his party were travelling along the road when suddenly a light brighter than the sun shot down from heaven and surrounded them. Terrified, Paul fell to the ground. He heard a voice say, *"Saul, Saul, why do you persecute me?"* *"Who are you Lord?"*, Saul asked. The voice answered, *"I am Jesus, whom you are persecuting."* (ACTS 9:4-5) The men with him stood speechless, hearing the voice, but seeing nothing. Paul was blind when he staggered to his feet, and they led him by the hand into Damascus. There he stayed in the house of a certain man by the name of Judas, on the street called Straight, and refused to eat or drink for three days. Then came a man known as Ananais and said, *"Brother Saul, the Lord Jesus, who appeared to you on the road as you were coming here - has sent me so that you may see again and be filled with the Holy Spirit."* (ACTS 9:17) Paul recovered his sight, arose and was baptised.

Men have puzzled over the conversion of Paul from that day to this present day. But Paul's conversion, however it may have happened, is certainly the most outstanding event in the history of the early church. Paul joined the disciples in Damascus and began to preach in the synagogues, saying that Jesus was truly the Son of God.

Paul's conversion, however had come too suddenly, he had not prepared for it, and he needed time to adjust himself to his new faith. The teachings of Christ could not have been difficult for him to accept, since they were based on the Scriptures, and were much like the teachings of Hillel, the famous Pharisee teacher.

Hillel, like Jesus, taught that the real heart of religion could be found in the two great commandments - to love God, and to love your neighbour. But the resurrection and all that it meant was new to Paul. He withdrew from society and lived for a time as a hermit in a desert area called Arabia.

When he felt ready to continue his ministry, he returned to Damascus and began preaching again in the synagogues. Some Jews considered him a traitor to his people and made plans to kill him. They posted guards at all the city gates to prevent his escape. The Christians, who were warned in time, took Paul by night and lowered him over the city wall in a basket. Paul made his way to Jerusalem to see Peter and the other Apostles who had known Jesus, personally. There were many questions he wanted to ask about the man (Jesus), who had given his life on the cross. But in Jerusalem the Christians avoided him. To them he was still Saul the persecutor. One man, Barnabas, came to his aid, and told them how Paul had been converted and had preached in the synagogues of Damascus.
Paul began to preach in Jerusalem. It was not long before he was in trouble again. He may have been to bold in his

preaching, for he offended so many Jews that the brethren feared for his life and sent him back to his home city of Tarsus. While he was there, according to tradition, his family and friends turned against him because he attempted to convert them. Paul had less success in his missionary work among the Jews, than did other brethren of the church.

The others used tact and patience, and they linked up the Gospel with their Jewish faith in such a way, that people could carry on with their old religion and be good Christians at the same time.

PAUL'S MISSIONS TO THE GENTILES

Paul believed the resurrection had changed everything. It proved to him that the Son of God, had suffered and died on the cross to was away the sins of the world. He believed that Christ, was the Way, the Truth, and the Light of the world who could give Life.

Paul's conversion had given him an entirely new outlook on life and religion. It had made him a different person. He said:

"Therefore, if anyone is in Christ, he is a new creation; the old has gone, the new has come!" (2 Cor 5:17)

The old laws and rituals of the Jewish religion were therefore no longer of any importance.

Not usually a tactful man, Paul refused to compromise with his new faith. He had to speak out. When he preached to the Jews he made it clear that the new faith had taken the place of the old. This, to the Jews, was an unbearable insult. Paul was asking them to turn their backs on the faith for which Jews had been fighting and dying for centuries.

Paul soon joined Barnabas, who had been placed in charge of the thriving new church in Antioch. For a year they carried on missionary work there.

A famine in Judea prompted the Christians in Antioch to take up a collection for the needy brethren. Barnabas and Paul were appointed to deliver the donations to the church at Jerusalem. In the Holy City they found the church in serious difficulty. King Herod Agrippa, trying to please the Jews, had launched a campaign of persecution against the Christians. Most of them were in hiding. James, the brother of John, had been beheaded. Peter was in prison at the time, but later managed to escape and leave the city. So many Christians fled from Jerusalem during the persecution, that the church there had never recovered its strength. Its influence faded in time, and Antioch became the centre of the Christian world.

Paul and Barnabas returned to Antioch and made ready for the first of several great missionary journeys, to bring the gospel of Jesus Christ to the world of the Gentiles. They set out in the year 45 A.D, and went first to the island of Cyprus. Then they crossed to the mainland of Asia Minor, and continued on over the mountains of Pisidia, to a country town, which also happened to be called Antioch. Paul preached there in the synagogue on the Sabbath. The Gentiles asked him to preach to them on the following Sabbath, which he did. He attracted such a large audience that the Jewish community became envious and turned against him. Paul told them, "It was necessary that the Word of God should be spoken to you first; but since you reject it, and judge yourselves unworthy of everlasting life, behold, we turn to the Gentiles. "For so the Lord has commanded us: saying...."*I have set you as a light to the Gentiles, that you should be for salvation to the ends of the earth.'"* When the Gentiles heard this, they were glad "and glorified the Word of the Lord". (ACTS 13: 46-48) NKJV*

But, the Jews went to the chief men of the town and had Paul and Barnabas, driven from the region. The two continued on foot for three or four days and came to Iconium, where they had limited success with the Jews. They converted so many Gentiles that they stayed there for sometime, and again Jews forced them to leave. They went to Lystra, some eighteen miles away. They had not been there long before Jews from Iconium arrived and organised the local Jews against them. Paul was caught, dragged out of the city, stoned and left for dead. The Christians, secretly brought him back into the town, and treated his wounds.

Undiscouraged, Paul and Barnabas went next to Derbe, and founded a church there. In spite of the danger, they went back to Lystra, and to each of the other towns to help with the new churches ordination of priests. They also preached in Perge, and finally returned by ship to their head-quarters in the city of Antioch. They were still there a year later, when Christian Jews came from Jerusalem, and told the Gentile brethren:

"Unless you are circumcised according to the custom of Moses, you cannot be saved." (ACTS 15 v 1) NKJV*

The Gentiles were greatly upset. They saw no reason why they should have to follow religious practices of the Jewish faith.

Barnabas and Paul, sided with the Gentiles. The question was so important that Paul and Barnabas, and others, decided to have it considered by the elders and apostles of the church of Jerusalem. The meeting in the Holy City in the year 48 A.D or 49 A.D, was the first council of the Christian Church. The elders in Jerusalem believed that Christian Jews should be required to carry out all obligations of their Jewish religion; but they had never been able to take a firm position regarding the Gentile Christians. One group held that the laws of Moses were binding upon the Gentiles, and the other group said, they were not.

Paul was anxious to have the question settled. He believed that the future of the church hung in the balance. Many Gentiles would not want to join the church if they had to accept the Jewish faith and the Law along with it. In that case, Christianity would always be merely another Jewish sect. Paul felt that if the Christian Jews wished to continue the practices of the Jewish faith, they should be allowed to do so. But he argued that the purpose of the laws of Moses, was to prepare the way for the coming of Christ. After the death and resurrection of Christ the laws had been fulfiled. They ceased to have any real importance and were therefore no longer binding upon anyone. There should be no distinctions between Christians, he said. They were all children of God. Once people had been baptised and had accepted Christ they were all the same. He said, *"There is neither Jew nor Greek, slave nor free, male nor female; for you are all one in Christ Jesus."* (GALATIANS 3: 28)

Salvation through Christ was for all people Paul declared. He had opened the door to the world of the Gentiles, and he wanted to continue working with them. He saw Christianity as a faith for all nations. The Jews who argued against him, were not thinking selfishly of themselves. Their concern was for the Jews as a people. They knew that if Paul's view was accepted, the Jews would feel that the religion of their fathers was being threatened. They could not accept Christ on that basis, and the end result would be that salvation through Christ would be denied to them. When all those who wished to speak had been heard, Peter stood up and announced the decision: *"Brethren, you know that a good while ago God chose among us, that by my mouth the Gentiles should hear the word of the gospel and believe. So God, who knows the heart …. Made no distinction between us and them, purifying their hearts by faith. Now therefore, why do you test God by putting a yoke on the neck of the disciples which neither our fathers nor we were able to bear….?"* (ACTS 15: v 7,9,10. NKJV)

Paul returned to Antioch with an official letter informing the Gentiles that they were not bound by the laws of Moses. But Paul's victory was not complete. Nothing had been decided about the Christian Jews. Were they still required to live according to the law of Moses? The question came up a short time later while Peter was present in Antioch. Peter always associated freely with the Gentiles and ate with them whenever he was from Jerusalem. But a party of very strict Christian Jews arrived from the Holy City and refused to associate with the Gentile members of the church, or to eat with them. Peter apparently found himself in an embarrassing position. A sudden change came over him, and he stopped associating with the

Gentiles. His influence was so great that Barnabas and many others began following his example. The Gentiles could not help notice the change. They were being shoved to one side, avoided, as if they were second-class Christians. Paul was furious. He recognised it as an attempt to push the Gentiles out and to keep Christianity a Jewish sect. He scolded Peter in public, and reminded him that salvation came through Jesus Christ, and not through following the Law. Peter quickly agreed. He told the people that there was no longer any reason for Christian Jews and Gentiles to be divided. They were all of one faith and could associate freely and eat together, for the laws of Moses were not binding upon any of them.

This decision finally put to rest the most critical problem faced by the young church. It doomed the hopes of those who wanted to keep Christianity a Jewish sect. It increased the opposition of the Jews to Christianity. But for Paul it meant that Christianity was for all people, all nations, a universal church.

PAUL'S SECOND MISSION

Paul's reception in Athens was unlike anything he had so far experienced. It was not the Jews that troubled him there. His visit probably took place in the year 50. Athens had long since passed her days of glory, and most of the city lay in ruins. But the place was crowded with students and people of culture and learning, who spent much of their time arguing philosophy and playing games. When they heard that a missionary was preaching in the synagogues, they were amused and asked each other. *"What is this babbler trying to say?"* (ACTS 17:18)

Paul preached to them on Mars' hill saying: *"Men of Athens! ....*
I perceive that in all things you are very religious, ... I even

found an altar with this inscription: TO THE UNKNOWN GOD. Therefore, the One whom you worship without knowing , Him I proclaim to you." (ACTS 17: 22-23 NKJV)

He told them how God had created the Heavens and the Earth, and all things, and tried to persuade them with skill and logic. But when he mentioned that Jesus had been raised from the dead, they laughed, jeered and mocked him.

Defeated in Athens, Paul went to Corinth, a city, a melting pot of shame and sin. It was a city in which the Corinthian people worshiped money and the kinky things it could buy. Money flowed freely, for Corinth straddled one of the Roman empires most vital trade routes. For their religious ideal, the fun-loving Corinthians adopted Venus, the goddess of love. And a temple built in her honour employed more than a thousand prostitutes. In the ancient world, the whole city of Corinth was best known for its prostituted lifestyle. Due to all these influences, Corinth loomed to Paul as the one city "least likely to convert" to the Christian faith. Yet, he met with incredible success that the church he established there became his favourite. He preached in Corinth for eighteen months and converted many, even Crispus, a leader of the synagogue. Leaving Silas and Timothy behind to carry on the work, Paul crossed the Aegean Sea again, landed in Ephesus, on the coast of Asia Minor, and sailed from there to Caesera. He reported on his mission in Jerusalem and then returned to Antioch.

His third missionary journey began a few weeks later. This time he took Titus as his companion. Again Paul visited all the churches in Asia Minor and then went on to Ephesus. The greatest port in Asia Minor, Ephesus was known as the pagan religious centre. The famous temple of Diana, one of the wonders of the ancient world, was located there, and attracted many pilgrims from other foreign lands during festival days. Paul remained in Ephesus approximately three years, supporting himself and his company by working at his trade, as a tent-maker. At first he preached in the synagogues, but soon began teaching daily in a private class-room provided by one of his converts. It was in Ephesus that Paul wrote some of his letters to the Galatians and the Corinthians. He won so many converts in Ephesus, that he all but ruined the business of those who made and sold images of the goddess Diana and small models of the temple. The silversmiths stirred up the people and caused so much confusion and bitterness, that Paul thought it best to leave the city.

He crossed over to Europe again and visited the young churches in Macedonia. He continued on into Greece and spent the winter in Corinth. About this time he wrote his famous Epistle to the Romans, in which he explained the Christian faith. It is recognised as one of the finest explanations of the faith ever written.

Literary types are often asked questions like this: "If you were marooned on a deserted island, what one book would you take along with you?" The majority would probably ask for a Bible. If asked the same question about a single book of the Bible, the majority of Christians would choose Romans. In Paul's letter to the Romans, he confessed that *"he longed to see"* and visit the Christian community in Rome. (ROMANS 1:11)

Paul's third great missionary journey ended with his arrival in Jerusalem in A.D 57. He was given a tumultuous welcome by the elders of the church. They advised him to go through the rite of purification and then appear in the temple, so that the Jews would have a better opinion of him. Paul followed their advice. But when he entered the Temple, he was recognised by certain Jews from Asia Minor. They pointed him out to other Jews, and they all rushed at him. So bitter was their hatred for Paul, that the Jewish mob even fought amongst themselves to get their hands on him. They dragged him into the street and would have killed him had not the Roman guards come quickly to his rescue.

The noisy mob followed the Romans as they took Paul to Antonia fortress. The chief captain, confused by their bitterness, had Paul taken inside and ordered him beaten so they could get the truth out of him. Paul protested. "Was it lawful to beat a Roman citizen before he had been sentenced?" A Roman citizen! The captain was very surprised when he heard Paul say that. Anyone who mistreated a citizen could be punished for it. The captain decided to hold Paul in prison, so that the Jews could bring formal charges against him.

Word came the following day that forty Jews had taken an oath not to eat or drink, until they had killed Paul. They head planned an ambush for him. To protect Paul, the captain sent him by night to Caesarea under a strong armed escort, and turned him over to Felix, the Roman governor. The Jews came from the Holy City and accused Paul of many things, but failed to prove anything against him. Felix held Paul for over two years, probably hoping Paul would offer money for his release.

Many of Paul's friends came to visit him in prison. According to tradition, Luke saw him often, and may have been gathering material during this period before writing the third gospel. After two years Felix was replaced by Festus. The new governor, wishing to please the Jews, asked Paul if he would return to Jerusalem and stand trial there. Paul refused, for he feared another Jewish ambush. He appealed as a roman citizen to Ceasar. This was a right that could not be denied. He would have to be tried in Rome, and Festus had to put the charges down in writing.

When King Agrippa 11 came for a visit, Paul was brought before him. He made such an able defence that Agrippa said to Festus, "This man could have been set free if he had not appealed to Ceasar."

In the fall of 59, Paul and some other prisoners were turned over to a Roman officer named Julius, who placed them on a sailing ship bound for Myra in Lycia. With Paul were two of his most faithful friends, Luke and Aristarchus. At Myra the prisoners were transferred to a ship bound for Italy. The wind held them back for many years, but they finally reached Fair Havens -- on the island of Crete. As they continued on their journey they were caught in a great storm, and were tossed about by the violent storm for fourteen days, with no sight of sun or stars by which to steer. On the fourteenth night they approached land. They did not know where they were. In the morning they drove the ship aground, and it soon began to break up under the pounding of the waves. Julius, the Roman Officer, ordered all those who could swim to jump overboard and make for shore. The others followed, clinging to boards and floating debris of the ship, and in time they all landed safely. They were told that they had landed on the island of Malta. There they remained for three months. They continued their journey on a ship named Castor and Pollux, which finally carried them up to Puteoli, in the Bay of Naples.

They found a Christian community at Puteoli, and Paul persuaded Julius to remain there a week so that he could preach the gospel. Meanwhile, word was sent to Rome of Paul's coming. When the journey was continued, many Christians from Rome came out along the Appian Way to greet him. Paul arrived in Rome probably early in March of the year 60, was allowed to rent a private house and live there by himself, with only a soldier to guard him.

His friends were free to come and go. Luke and Aristarchus kept him company. There is a tradition that Luke was then writing his Gospel and the Book of Acts. Timothy was there and Mark, who may have been writing the second Gospel at that time. With all these men to help him, Paul must have taken an active part in the affairs of the Christian communities in Rome. He converted many who came to his house, and even some of the soldiers who guarded him. He made his influence felt in the outside world as well, for he continued writing letters to the churches he founded, and to various individuals. His epistle to the Philippians in Macedonia and one to the Colossians in

Phrygia, were probably written during this time. *"And he lived there two whole years at his own expense and welcomed all who came to him, preaching the kingdom of God and teaching about the Lord Jesus Christ quite openly and unhindered."* (italics mine). The Acts of the Apostles comes to a sudden end with these above lines, and nothing positive is known about the last years of Paul's remarkable life.

According to one tradition, Paul was released in the year 62, made a missionary journey to Spain, and may have also visited Crete, Corinth, Ephesus, and Nicopolis. He was arrested a second time and brought back to Rome, where he was kept in a damp cell in the Tullianum jail. There is another tradition that Paul was held prisoner for about four years and then was beheaded on the Ostian Way in 64, at the time when the Roman Emperor Nero, was persecuting the Christians. According to this tradition, Peter was crucified upside down in Rome at the same time.

Paul, the apostle of the Gentiles, is considered the greatest missionary of all time. It was largely due to his efforts and influence that the Christian faith broke away from the laws of Moses, and became a world-wide religion, instead of a Jewish sect. It's rather uncanny, that the one single person in all history, by personal education, theological inclination, and racial motivation, Paul of Tarsus, in 13 letters did more than any single believer here on earth to reveal the memory of Jesus Christ, after his dramatic conversion from persecuting Christians of "the Way".

WITNESSING FOR CHRIST

THE GREAT COMMISSION

He told them, "GO into all the world and preach the Good News to everyone, everywhere."

(Mark 16:15)
New Living Bible

As Christians we have a moral obligation to God, and part of our response to Him, as He reveals His being and divine nature to us on a daily basis, is our making Him known in a world in which He is widely ignored or rejected. This involves spreading the knowledge of God, throughout the world, both geographically and culturally, by our prayers, the investment of our church's resources and our personal witness.

The call to witness lay at the heart of Jesus Christ's final instructions to the apostles in the Book of Acts chapter 1 and verse 8. It was here at *'Pentecost'*, that just a handful of disciples set about their task. Since apostle literally means **"sent one"**, we as God's apostles, His set apart ones, His witnesses are authorised bearers of the Gospel, and hence we have a duty, a mission. This great mission that every Christian believer has been ordained to do, is to be a witness to the resurrection power and ministry of our LORD JESUS CHRIST.

Evangelism (Witnessing), is not just using words to preach to other people, it's a commitment in bringing people of all nations into the knowledge of who God is; it's sharing our faith with others in love. In the Book of Philemon chapter 1 and verse 6,

Apostle Paul writes *"I pray that you may be active in sharing your faith, so that you will have a full understanding of every good thing we have in Christ. "* (NIV).

Is Witnessing really necessary?

Psalm 107:2 *Let the redeemed of the LORD say so, whom He hath redeemed from the hand of the enemy.*

Mark 16:15 *And He said unto them, "Go ye into all the world, and preach the Gospel ("Good News") to every creature.*

God commands us as Christian believers, to tell others about what He has done.

Mark 1:17 *And Jesus said unto them, "Come ye after Me, and I will make you to become fishers of men."*

Acts 10:42 *And He commanded us to preach unto all the people, and to testify that it is He which was ordained of God to be the Judge of quick and dead.*

Evangelism is an intrinsic part of being Christ's followers (believers).

2 Kings 7:9 *Then they said to one another, we do not well: this day is a day of good tidings, and we hold our peace: if we tarry till the morning light, some mischief will come upon us: now therefore come, that we may go and tell the king's household.*

It is not right for us to hold back, to keep the Good News to ourselves. Our witness is the only way some people will ever hear the 'Salvation' story of our Lord Jesus Christ.

Romans 10:14 *How then shall they call on Him in whom they have not believed? and how shall they believe in Him of whom they have not heard? and how shall they hear without a preacher?*

The only way that people can be saved, is by hearing and believing the message of Good News that we have.

Ezekiel 3:18 *When I say unto the wicked, Thou shalt surely die; and thou givest him not warning, nor speakest to warn the wicked from his wicked way, to save his life; the same wicked man shall die in his iniquity; but his blood will I require at thine hand.*

If we keep silent about the things of Christ, we will be subject to God's punishment.

Jude 1:23 *And others save with fear, pulling them out of the fire; hating even the garment spotted by the flesh.*

WE must as Believers rescue others from the flames of judgement.

What should my witnessing include?
Exodus 18:9 *And Jethro rejoiced for all the goodness which the LORD had done to Israel, whom he had delivered out of the*

hand of the Egyptians.

John 9:25 *He answered and said, Whether he be a sinner or no, I know not: one thing I know, that, whereas I was blind, now I see.*

Your witness should include telling others how God has rescued you and healed your sin-blinded heart.

Psalm 28:6 *Blessed be the LORD, because He hath heard the voice of my supplications.*

Proclaim how God has answered your prayers.

Psalm 30:3 *O LORD, thou hast brought up my soul from the grave: thou hast kept me alive, that I should not go down to the pit.*

Explain to others how God has saved you from spiritual death.

Acts 4:33 *And with great power gave the apostles witness of the resurrection of the Lord Jesus: and great grace was upon them all.*

Be sure to tell others the news of Christ's resurrection.

Acts 10:42 *And He commanded us to preach unto the people, and to testify that it is He which was ordained of God to be the Judge of quick and dead.*

Don't be afraid to warn people about the coming judgement by the living Christ.

1 Peter 3:15 *But sanctify the Lord God in your hearts: and be ready always to give an answer to every man that asketh you a reason of the hope that is in you with meekness and fear.*

Be ready to explain to others why you have hope.

1 John 1:2 *(For the life was manifested, and we have seen it, and bear witness, and shew unto you that eternal life, which was with the Father, and was manifested unto us;)*

Tell others the "good news" that eternal life is only found in Christ.

1 Corinthians 2:2 *For I determined not to know anything among you, save Jesus Christ, and Him crucified.*

Tell others how Jesus died on the Cross to take away our sins.

Luke 24:47 *And that repentance and remission of sins should be preached in His name among all nations, beginning at Jerusalem.*

Explain the message of repentance, forgiveness, and reconciliation with God.

Romans 10:9 *That if thou shalt confess with thy mouth the Lord Jesus, and shalt believe in thine heart that God hath* *raised Him from the dead, thou shalt be saved.*

Stress the importance the need to confess Christ as Lord and believe in His resurrection.

1 Thessalonians 1:5 *For our gospel came not unto you in word only, but also in power, and in the Holy Ghost, and in much assurance; as ye know what manner of men we were among you for your sake.*

How you live as a Christian is an important element of your witnessing for Christ Jesus.

Daniel 12: 3 *And they that be wise shall shine as the brightness of the firmament; and they that turn many be righteousness as the stars for ever and ever.*

This is my prayer for every Christian believer, that you will be used by Almighty God, to bring many souls to the knowledge of Christ Jesus' salvation power, mercy, truth, grace and unconditional love - AMEN!

"THE coming of the LORD is bound up with the Universal spread of the Gospel!"

Three Effective Methods Of Evangelism

In the 15th chapter of Luke's gospel, Jesus spoke of the parable of the **one** lost sheep and the **one** lost coin that were lost. And, the attitudes of the sheep owner and the woman are very noteworthy. But, all their attention, energy, and resources were solely directed at or channelled towards that which was lost. The life of Jesus Christ, clearly reveals to us this outward-looking mentality. It tells us Christians something about His soul-winning strategy.

Have you ever wondered why the great Apostle Paul, was so great and successful in his ministry of Evangelism?
He had a **strategy** a **plan**.
What was Paul's strategy? Well, in the Book of Romans chapter 15, and verse 20, we get some clue to Paul's great vision. *"Yea, so have I strived to preach the gospel, not where Christ was named, lest I should build upon another man's foundation."*

Paul's focus was always outward --- to the next town, city and village. So as believers, shouldn't this be our aim as the Body of Christ, to witness for Christ Jesus?
3 Effective Methods of Evangelism:-
o   **Street Evangelism** --- 'one-on-one' **or** 'face-to-face' **contact**.
o   **Revival Crusade or Convention.**
o   **Gospel Concert.**

Street Evangelism, I believe to be number one as an effective method of Evangelism for a church close to all amenities. Firstly, it gives every Christian the opportunity to share/testify to the "Gospel" of Jesus Christ. There are I believe to be 20 things we need to focus on, before any member of a church participates in Street Evangelism.

Make a definite time and day for soul-winning; Be soul conscious: have in your heart and your mind that your a soul-winner, and that everyone you meet is a potential believer; be neat in your appearance and watch your breath! ; Carry a small pocket Bible (a rather large one can be intimidating!); Go out in two's --- this was Christ's recommendation, and it's good to have moral support; Pray as you go (very important), asking God for boldness, wisdom, insight, discernment, a word of knowledge; Drop all religious jargons! Example --- are you justified? ; Don't be confrontational; Be complimentary; Very, very important --- be a very good listener; Talk one at a time; Stay on the subject of Salvation; Show the person that he/she is lost without Christ; Ask important questions (e.g. 'If you die today, do you expect to go to heaven?") ; Memorise and use these Scriptures, mainly found in the Book of Romans.

**** Romans 3:23; 6:23; 5:8; 10:9-13 and John 3:16 ****

Ask to pray with the person --- lead him/her through the sinners prayer; Invite the person to Church and volunteer to accompany the person for the first Sunday service; Check on the person later, before church, and go together if possible; Continue praying for the person in your private prayer time.

Revival Crusade:- the second effective method of Evangelism. This programme of action involves more careful planning by a Church. Time/Date is very important. Your Revival Crusade should not coincide with any other events which may be taking place within your community on the same day. Try to plan well in advance, this gives the church time to focus on promotional coverage. Research the area you live in to see what age group or ethnic background, your church is specifically targeting. The "message", or title of the Revival Crusade is equally important. Do you stage the event within your church, or have an open-air crusade, or seek better premises? For example, if your church decides to stage a presentation of the Gospel, through Drama, does the church have the facilities and space? Will your church be requiring the services of International renowned speakers? Travel arrangements --- Is the Revival Crusade, close to bus services or public transport (train or underground stations)? How long is the Revival Crusade for (how many days)?

Admission should always be free.

Lastly, *pray* and *fast* very important.

Gospel Concert:- Again, the time and date if possible must not clash with any other event taking place within your community. promotion of the event, using all forms of the media tends to get people's attention. Choice of Gospel Singer or Singers. Do you employ the services of a household name in the Christian music scene from another country? Does the church have the sufficient funds or space to hold such an event using a Gospel singer who is known? Do you hold the event free of charge or ask monies, and how much should you charge for entry? Is the area where your church is situated, does it have a low/high unemployment rate? Do you target the young or old, or both?

For any church to be effective in Evangelism within its local community, they must adopt strategies, ideas, and plans, such as the three I have listed for you and the church you attend. These three might not necessarily work for your Church but, I can boast from personal experience as an Evangelist and Pastor, that they are I believe to be the most successful in witnessing and, in developing church growth considerably within a local community.

How Can I Share My Christian Faith Without An Argument?

The Approach
o   Do you have any kind of spiritual belief?
o   To you who is Jesus?
o   Do you think there is a Heaven and hell?
o   If you died right now, where do you think you would go?
o   If what you believe were not true, would you want to know it?

The Close
o   Are you a sinner?
o   Do you want forgiveness of sins?
o   Do you believe that Jesus Christ, died on a Cross and rose again?
o   Are you willing to surrender your life to Christ?
o   Are you ready to invite Jesus into your heart and into your life?

REMEMBER:- It is the Holy Spirit who does the convincing and the convicting. You just be silent and continue to pray, and let the Spirit of God, do His work! It's not by your power, or your might or strength but, by His Spirit, saith the LORD of Hosts!! -AMEN.

WITNESS BEARING
(ACTS 1:8)

"But ye shall receive power, after that the Holy Ghost is come upon you: and ye shall be witnesses unto Me both in Jerusalem, and in all Judea, and in Samaria, and unto the uttermost part of the earth."

o   What is it to be a witness? ------------------- EVIDENCE
o   Where is the place? -------------------- BEGIN AT HOME
o   What is the power? --------------------THE HOLY SPIRIT

WITNESSES TO CHRIST

o   The Father, ----------------------------------- John 8:18
o   The Son, -------------------------------------- John 8:18
o   The Holy Spirit, ------------------------------ John 15:26
o   The Holy Scriptures, ------------------------- John 5:39
o   John the Baptist, ----------------------------- John 1:15
o   The Works of Christ, ------------------------- John 5:36
o   The Prophets, --------------------------------- Acts 10:43
o   The Believer, ---------------------------------- Acts 1:8

As a Christian, do we have the right to persuade people of other religions to become Christians?

Whatever answer we think is right, the first thing to be clear about is our own attitude towards people of other faiths. This is important whether we meet them in this country or overseas.

Respect for other religions

A right attitude begins by our recognising that they have a faith in their religion as strong or as weak as our own. They live by what they believe, or fail to do so, just as we do. Next, it is important to realise that, as far as this country is concerned, they are a minority group. As such, they feel themselves threatened. This makes them stick very closely together, and makes them very suspicious of any approach by Christians.

This attitude of theirs is wholly understandable and deserves our sympathy. Very few of them want to be assimilated to our way of life. They value their traditional culture. And in the culture of the Muslim or the Hindu or the Sikh or the Buddhist, religion enters into every part of life. For a Sikh, for instance, the wearing of a turban is part of his culture and his religion, something which our bureaucrats do not understand. With us, the wearing of a bowler hat or a cloth cap has nothing to do with our religion. For a Sikh, what he wears on his head really does matter.

Again, marriage traditions in the Hindu community and among Muslims are very different from ours. The freedom between the sexes which we enjoy, they view with great misgivings. Women's Lib is not a movement they either approve of or understand. That does not mean they are stupid.

How to treat 'strangers'
Our most important task as a Christian believer, at all times is to understand and respect the convictions of these 'strangers' who are our fellow-citizens. In the Holy Bible, there is quite a lot about the way to treat strangers. **(Exodus 2:21; Leviticus 19:33-34; and Deuteronomy 10:18-19),** are just three out of many references which show the ideal set before the people of Israel. They did not live up to it always, any more than we do. But we, as Christians, cannot have lower ideals.

(Matthew 25:35-43), has something very important to say about strangers. **(Hebrews 13:2)**, actually tells us to entertain them. If we go abroad, and live in a country where we are aliens, and are often only a tiny handful of strangers in a Muslim, Hindu, or Buddhist culture, we soon realise the importance of these biblical guide-lines. When we ourselves are outsiders, the advice of **(Deuteronomy 10:19)**, *"Love the stranger"* sounds good! And it applies the other way round.

We will never be able to think straight about the religious faith of other men until we get our attitude to them right. Only then can we begin to look for an answer to our question.

Persuasion
What do we really mean by persuading people of other religions to become Christians?

What kind of Christians do we want them to become? Are we sure that we know? Pentecostals, Methodists, Baptists, Presbyterian's, Anglicans, Roman Catholics --- all these are Christians, but the ways in which they express there faith and organise their common life are, in some respects, very different. Are we quite sure that any one of them is so absolutely right that we can ask the man or woman of another religion to choose, and be quite sure he/she will make the choice we think is the right one?

Obviously our question raises a lot of other questions. But that is not the end of the matter. We live in a world full of suffering and sorrow, a world in which there is so much evil, a world in which death can be very sudden, in which dying can take such very unpleasant forms. Now, if we ourselves know someone who can help men and women to cope with this kind of world, who can give them hope and courage and joy (an abundant life in other words), surely we ought at least to try to effect an introduction.

Persuading is always in danger of being a form of pressure. But simply to tell of our own experience (Testimony), of Jesus Christ as a Saviour who can meet and supply all our needs, is quite different. We report what we know, we encourage our stranger-friend to read, perhaps, St John's Gospel or one of the others. And we leave Jesus to make His own impact. Of course, we will pray for this stranger-friend of ours, believing God for their salvation. We will also pray that our own lives may show to the world what Jesus Christ has done for us. But the other man, the other woman, is left free to say 'Yes' or 'No.'

This is the real Christian duty, whether we do it in our own street, or in America, or in Italy or Nigeria or anywhere else. To know Jesus Christ and what He has done for us, and is still doing for us, and not to share the "good news" with others is selfishness. Not, only is it selfishness but God has commanded each and everyone of us believers, in His Word to go and tell some one about His unconditional love, His grace, His mercy, His faithfulness, His Salvation power. We are supposed to be *'watchmen'* for Christ, in accordance to the Holy Scriptures. In particular, the Book of Ezekiel chapter 3 and verse 18, gives us a clear warning and to the unbeliever, that we will be held accountable if we do not witness our faith.

"When I say unto the wicked, Thou shalt surely die; and thou givest him not warning, nor speakest to warn the wicked from his wicked way, to save his life; the same wicked man shall die in his iniquity; but his blood will I require at thine hand."

Evangelism consists of fallen men speaking the "good news" to fallen men, or, as someone has put it, *'one beggar telling another beggar where bread is to be found'*. The church cannot wait to be perfect before proclaiming Her message. We preach the Gospel not from a moral eminence but out of sympathy. Of course our voice will be heeded much more when we speak from holiness than when we are compromised by worldliness, but whatever our imperfections we must not remain silent. It would be a greater hypocrisy to have the Gospel of Salvation and to keep it to ourselves --- so friend in Christ, do as God has commanded you --- **GO NOW , and tell someone the good news about Jesus Christ !!**

WE MUST GIVE SERVICE TO GOD

o   **The Need of Service**

Therefore said He unto them, The harvest truly is great, but the labourers are few: pray ye therefore the Lord of the harvest, that He would send forth labourers into His harvest. (Luke 10:2). *Say not ye, there are yet four months, and then cometh harvest? behold, I say unto you, Lift up your eyes, and look on the fields; for they are white already to harvest* (John 4:35).

o   **The Call and Response**

And I heard the voice of the Lord, saying, Whom shall I send, and who will go for us? Then I said I, here am I; send me. (Isaiah 6:8).

And He saith unto them, Follow Me, and I will make you fishers of men. And they straightway left their nets, and followed Him. (Matthew 4: 19-20).

But what think ye? A certain man had two sons; and he came to the first, and said, Son, go work today in my vineyard. (Matthew 21:28).

o   **A Voluntary Offering**

Lord, what wilt thou have me do? (Acts 9:6).

o   **The Spirit of Service**

Serve the Lord with gladness: come before His presence with singing. (Psalm 100:2).

And the seventy returned with joy, saying, Lord, even the devils are subject unto us through thy name. (Luke 10:17).

o	**Motivated by Love**

And though I bestow all my goods to feed the poor, and though I give my body to be burned, and have not charity [love], it profiteth me nothing. (1 Corinthians 13:3).

For, brethren, ye have been called unto liberty [freedom]; only use not liberty [freedom] for an occasion to the flesh, but by love serve one another. (Galatians 5:13).

o	**The measure of Greatness**

Whosoever will be great among you, let him be your minister; and whosoever will be chief among you, let him be your servant: even as the Son of man came not to be ministered unto, but to minister, and to give His life a ransom for many. (Matthew 20:26-28)

o	**Faith Justified by Service**

But wilt thou know, O vain man, that faith without [apart from] works is dead [barren] ? Ye see then how that by works a man is justified, and not by faith only, for as the body without the spirit is dead, so faith without works is dead also. (James 2: 20,24,26).

o	**A Saving Service**

To the weak became I as weak, that I might gain the weak: I am made all things to all men that I might by all means save some. (1 Corinthians 9:22).
Let him know, that he which converteth the sinner from the error of his way shall save a soul from death, and shall hide a multitude of sins. (James 5:20).

o   **Acknowledged by Christ**

And the King shall answer and say unto them, Verily I say unto you, Inasmuch as ye have done it unto one of the least of these My brethren, ye have done it unto Me. (Matthew 25:10).

For whosoever shall give you a cup of water to drink in My name, because ye belong to Christ, verily I say unto you, he shall not lose his reward. (Mark 9:41).

o   **Reward of Faithful Service**

His lord said unto him, Well done, thou good and faithful servant: thou hast been faithful over a few things, I will make thee ruler over many things: enter thou into the joy of thy lord. (Matthew 25: 21).

And he that reapeth receiveth wages, and gathereth fruit unto life eternal: that both he that soweth and he that reapeth may rejoice together. (John 4:36).

And they that be wise shall shine as the brightness of the firmament; and they that turn many to righteousness as the stars for ever and ever. (Daniel 12:3).

**For he whom God hath sent
speaketh the words of God:
for God giveth not the Spirit
by measure unto him.**

(JOHN 3:34)

How Can I Break the Guilty Silence?

Why do we as Christian believers find it so difficult to break the silence about the best news and most important person the world has ever known?

Why is it so hard to say those first few words about the most important Person in my life?

Why do I hesitate to pass along the best news I have ever heard? Is there anything that will help me to do the very thing I want so much to do --- to tell others that I have found a way of surviving death, living forever, being forgiven of my sins and exploring the goodness of God forever. In many ways the church is not silent. The sounds of well-amplified music echo through its halls. Passionate sermons fill the sanctuary. Laughter and conversation flow into the parking lot. Yet, in the midst of all these sounds, there is a disturbing quiet. It's called *"our guilty silence"*.

All too often those of us who have so much to say to one another have little to say to those who desperately need what we have. Furthermore, we expect them to come to us when we should be going to them. The sad truth is, that all too often we (believers) are not carrying on the pattern of (ACTS); of reaching the downtrodden, the broken hearted --- with the "good news" of Jesus Christ.

In fact, we fail to reach either the rich or poor, the educated or the uneducated. While enjoying one another we are not reaching those *'lost souls'*, who still are as we once were --- without Christ. If so, this is **"our guilty silence"**.

My advice to you, is use the "Acts Strategy"
We as Believers in Christ, must learn to adopt the Book of Acts, if we aim to be good at witnessing or evangelising. The Book of Acts, is first and foremost a book of *'action'*. It gives us God's Sovereign plans in sharing the "good news", to all nations, all peoples, and how we as Christians can put them into practice. I pray you too, will adopt the **'Acts Strategy'**, and be a sold-out, soul winner for Christ Jesus, in His magnificent name !!! - AMEN.